For Us, The Sensitive

A Poetry Journal

Written by: Tumi Adegoroye

Copyrighted Material
All rights reserved.
ISBN: 9781673815092

For Us, The Sensitive

A collection of personal words, womanish thoughts and fragile feelings
by Tumi Adegoroye

Dedication

To the women in my life.

You never get tired of picking me up each time I fall.

I love you.

For Us, The Sensitive

For us whose generosity and love do not expire, we are essential to life, a gift to the world.

For Us, The Sensitive

Dear Sensitive,

Being as fragile as I am, I have come to understand that life cannot be always easy. This book was written as a form of journaling, which I find to be my healing power, a quench to my thirst and a resting place for my heart.

This book is a condensed form of some of my feelings.

A while ago, it felt as though chapter after chapter, as I moved through life, there was disappointment waiting for me. My heart was heavy, my soul was not ready, I felt abandoned and ignored.

It made me sad that my little issues influenced my emotions as if there were not millions of people all over the world with worse problems. Please, do not measure your/our pain by what others have experienced or are experiencing.

Writing this personal journal helped me understand the value of being a highly sensitive person. Being sensitive might seem "childish", but if you have tried to change this aspect of your life, and it does not seem to work, it might as well be a gift from God - for you to feel things, learn from the feelings and experiences, then be your own being regardless. Everyone has a sensitive side and when you tap into it, it does not make you weak...it makes you human. Our emotions run deep and that's not something to hide all the time.

This book might help you realize that these feelings are shared by so many despite feeling you are alone. For me, writing this book helped me realize that my fear of failure and loneliness is the only thing stopping me from being the best version of myself.

This journey is made for us to *learn* and *enjoy*. The pain is the lesson, deciding to learn from the pain is the growth. Growth is continuous, and when you know this, you might attain personal joy. I

For Us, The Sensitive

honestly have not reached the optimum level of personal joy, but I want to be responsible for my happiness throughout my lifetime.

Because of love, poetry and music I am able to survive. Because of good entertainment and art, I am able to live life knowing I am not alone, I can still smile and laugh. I can live knowing I have a gift to feel all sorts of things around me and I am thankful to God.

These are my feelings, but they might be yours too.

This book is for those who feel a little too much. It is for us, the sensitive.

~ *Chapters* ~

Fragile Feelings - 10

Womanish Thoughts - 41

Royal Reminders - 71

For Us, The Sensitive

~ *Fragile Feelings* ~

On the first day of spring
I listen to "everything is love"
Reminiscing on when
We were young
I still think of you
When it is full moon
While drinking freshly made wine
Under the stars.

These are the things
That remind me of you.

The One That Got Away

Journal entry i

there was a phase in my life where relationships
with my friends and family were at stake.
at this time, relationships were laid naked and bare
on the floor — we would ask each other, "are we
going to do this or not?" meaning — are we going
to let go or not? these were times when we all
changed as we grew; when some situations became
uneasy and uncomfortable.

bridges that were previously burnt down were built
up again.

these were moments when we came to each other
face to face and laid it all on the floor - all our
fears, demons, vulnerabilities and flaws.
were we willing to change, listen and understand
ourselves?
were we willing to love each other's true self?

there was sadness, along with anger and frustration.

we told each other everything, used all the words we knew, screamed louder than anything, as nothing was quiet.
i never knew that day would come because we thought it was all behind us, but see, people change and so do you.

this thing called love is not for the weak.

Sincerely, Tums
kisses!

For Us, The Sensitive

There you go,
Sharing the love I crave
And the pieces of you
That calm my aching heart
As if you weren't mine
Before the world's.

I don't blame you,
Who could ever let you go?

You are
The sweetest fruit I know
Your spirit like silk
And your courage — unmatched.
With your sparkling love
You care for me
Like the gatekeeper of my heart
My friend before my lover.

Loving you for a long time

Where did you come from?
You decided to come with me
On my journey,
Behind the wheel
Driving me crazy.

Can you slow down?
Take a break?
Or just leave?
You, the uninvited guest.

But sometimes
I do think
Maybe you are a part of me.
I want you gone
But sometimes
 you are right.

Constantly listening to you
As you sing in my ear
The tunes I want to hear,
My soul feels shaky
Is it me or is it you?

I run into hiding,
But your voice only gets louder.

Paranoia,
Who are you again?
What are you doing here?
Can you leave?
You've had enough of me
As I, of you.

Paranoia or Instincts

Thought i:

My heart sinks

At

The thought of him

Being with another lover.

For Us, The Sensitive

Our love was like a pink orange
It appeared to be charmingly sweet
Drooling in love and intimacy
Tickled with friendship and warmth
It seemed beautifully carved
And yet, pungent.

The true flavour of our love
Was like a grapefruit
Bitterly cold and sour
It seemed strong and harsh,
But we stayed
And endured the taste
Knowing the flavour wouldn't change.

It's such an amazement
That something can
Look so perfect,
And yet, taste acidic.

GrapeFruit

Leading me on
Because you want
To have your way
In my loving bed.

Toxic 101

For Us, The Sensitive

He left you
To make love with another
While you were still together.

Why carry the guilt?
It is his venom
That destroyed your love
And broke Cupid's bow.

With all the love you gave,
How dare you blame yourself
For someone else's poison?

Why won't you write me back?

i do think about you a lot
and i can't help but
wonder why you never write me back.
i wish you could see
how i am changing
i am patient now
i take time to listen
even when i want
to jump out and speak.
i'm changing.
but, why won't you write me back?
i know i told you to
"leave me alone"
and called you the worst
but, i am working on myself
and i want to do the work
because i see how i was wrong.
i wish you would write me back
so you'd see for yourself
that i'm different now.

For Us, The Sensitive

No to half love
Yes to good love
Love with effort
Love that is kind, patient,
Understanding and willing to grow
Love that might not be perfect
But is willing to work
Yes to good love
Love that is not greedy
A type of love that is honest
Even when it hurts
A godly love, a hopeful one
A love that is present, the type that evolves.

For Us, The Sensitive

Because it was the
Most patient love you
Had ever experienced,
You held on tight
You thought you would
Never be loved like that again
So, you acted like life depended on it.

Fear lies

Journal entry ii

Note to self

On days when you don't know exactly why you feel down, or you feel heavy in the heart and no matter what you hear, read or write, it doesn't get better - you need to take care of your
mind and act like it is an egg.
fragile, yet a whole life and a whole world.
you need to take deep breaths and
remember that you cannot avoid such days.

when a day like this comes, you must learn not to overthink situations.
you must learn to treat
yourself to a piece of cheesecake, work out and find joy in a piece of art; maybe music, movies or a painting.
you must learn to try
again the next day, and the next, and the next...

it will get better.

Sincerely, Tums
Kisses!

one thing i'm grateful for right now is the power i hold in my life.

i remember being sad most of last year - thinking my accomplishments were too small and falling into a state of depression and regret.

today, i'm glad i have the power to curate my life and mold my future the way i want.

even though the power i hold might be limited, i still have some agency to do things for myself.

on some days i am disgustingly moody, but i have the power to decide if i want to stay in that state of sadness - loathing in self-pity or burst with joy and gratefulness that i am alive.

In life, we have the choice to stay grateful.

a learned behaviour

> *you want children too,*
> *you also want a partner*
> *but you fear you will be*
> *like him, your first love...*
> *pushing beloveds away*
> *feeling guilt*
> *aware, but clueless*
> *present, but absent.*

Someone else is hurt,
Because you failed to do the work.
You did not stop bad habits
You did not take time to love yourself
You did not learn how to heal
You did not cater to your wounds.
So, you hurt others
While hurting yourself.

Yes, we do have feelings
And we should feel them.
However, you need to know
Not to use your feelings
As an excuse.
Sometimes we are hurting
Our loved ones
Without knowing it.

Guilty as charged

For Us, The Sensitive

We might find love
And sweet friendship
In places where
we might not search for it.
Sometimes it finds us
In strange places too.

And Oh! How beautiful it is.

Unexpected Love

I have never known this kind of love,
Love so brave,
Love so dynamic.
It changes but remains sweet love
Kind love,
Honest love,
Loyal.
So active and powerful.
Thank you for showing me what sisterhood truly is.

Sister sister

For Us, The Sensitive

Thought ii:

The love I receive from my family and friends,
 stops me from settling for shiftless love.
I wish you could love me the way they do, and
 better.

Thought iii:

I went from feeling something
Tangibly immeasurable for you
To feeling numb - nothing
Just emptiness
No bitterness, no sadness.
Just an empty space for you
A void space that needs no filling.

If you feel numb in some situations,
You are actually feeling something
Sometimes feeling nothing
Is feeling something
Sometimes numb feelings
Are stronger than tangible feelings.

Thought iv:

When I think about sensitive people, I think of strings attached to control a puppet.
For us sensitive people, the heart is the string.

It's difficult thinking without a heart, it's difficult not attaching things to the heart.
It's difficult making decisions without consulting the heart.
It's what has brought us this far, I also heard it's a super power.

May God help our soft hearts.

Poets are very similar to scientists.

They analyze and solve world issues with *words*.

> we're contemporary fairies,
> modern storytellers,
> different energies, with the same message.
> within - there's dark art and there's light.
> I am surprised the world cannot see that.

Photographers, writers, singers, models, creators, actresses, however you identify as an artist) you are a fairy - use your gift for good.

For Us, The Sensitive

Explaining something real
To someone who has
Refused to understand
Is like waiting for a seed
To germinate
When it has not even been planted.

Struggles of a minority

Journal entry iii

~~Lessons~~

It felt like he came into my life having the notion that since I hadn't experienced terrible trauma, I was living a life not worth being depressed about.

He thought he knew me so well.
He did not know what I had been through; all the guilt, pain and anger inside of me.

He hurt me as if he wanted to teach me a lesson,
As if he wanted to show me what pain felt like,
As if I hadn't felt it before.

Sincerely, Tums

For Us, The Sensitive

A letter to you...

Dear papi,

I fell for you without a thought, in the middle of summer.
Day after day I waited to see your face through the glass window and give you a hug.

At nighttime, we would talk on the phone from dusk to dawn, and even while we were away from each other, we were present.
Laughter and joy were our muse, and our hearts became light.

Even if I haven't heard from you in years, I miss you dearly.
I miss your laugh,
I miss your smile,
I miss your words, and most of all
I miss your soul.

Come over and bring some flowers

Watch me have a bubble bath with a glass of wine on the side
Let the candles burn while we watch Spike Lee movies during the snowstorm
Let's make love like we met yesterday
Let's talk about our plans and aspirations
Let's dance to afro soul and jazz
Let's fall in love like it's the middle of summer again.

Even if we left the love scene, I still crave your presence.

The love that i love is my soulmate

Love,
Tumi

for better or worse?

> You expect me not to
> Look for you,
> But you owe me the world
> And some more love.
> I'm back to collect
> What you promised me.

make a wish!

I wish for a lover that will always captivate me, one that accepts and loves my true self - I wish to be that lover too.
I wish for children that will be loving and better humans than I am.
I wish for a small life and a glorious effect.
I wish for my parents to be happy and at peace with life.
I wish for fulfillment and joy for my siblings.
I wish for more happy memories...for my family and friends to be successful.

My big dreams are my little wishes, I only want the simple things in life.

For Us, The Sensitive

~ Womanish Feelings ~
Also known as humanly feelings

Thought v:

You always wanted me to feel your presence, so you sent an angel to care for me.

Thank you, God.

- A Mother's Love

The structure of the world in her view

Designed to make her give, give, give
Give birth, give love, give all of her.

Structured to exploit her,
To break her bones
And burn her out.

Organized to make the most of her
Like a flourishing tree,
As if we don't know
What they do to trees.

But, she remains sweet and compassionate,
She is filled with love and light.
With drastic changes, she's uncomfortable.
Nonetheless, she adapts.

A woman listens
But also wants to be heard
She wants to be
She wants it all
She wants to be everything.

Sometimes ignorant of her power
Yet aware of the magic inside her.

Like a plant, she pulls to the sun
She represents light and energy
She has learnt the nature of the peacock
How it stands in its true self,
How it displays itself unapologetically.
It blossoms
Knowing it has the power to do so,
Not from anyone,
But from and for itself.
She knows playing small does not serve her,
So she dreams big.

For Us, The Sensitive

Understanding A Woman

Don't you understand?
Or have you forgotten so quickly?

Your heart is different,
You love differently,
Fail differently
Rise differently.

A human's power

For Us, The Sensitive

Telling me to smile,
Asking if my hair is mine.
When I speak up
You tell me to hold up,
Calling it a whine.

How else can she explain?
Her experience is different
The gaze on her is different,
She's delicate but bold.

Black women,
Mad magicians
With so much load
And lots of tricks.
Often misunderstood,
Impossible to understand.
Baffling beauty,
Shamed.

BlackWomenAreMadMagicians

she went to her God
and asked why feels everything;
the words of others, intense lights,
lingering feelings, her very own thoughts
recycling over and over,
making their names known to her.

God answered,
"you feel everything,
so your life can be whole again
as you tell your story."

Thought vi:

I am still learning to walk away when things are not right for me.
I am still learning to understand the difference between my instincts and paranoia.
I want to have the courage to walk away from all that does not serve my heart or better the world as a whole.

A letter to him:

I know the world has been unfair to you
And with so much knowledge about the world
You have chosen your little space
Where you can find comfort and sanity.
I see a kind man
Someone who has saved the lives of many
But has remained wounded in his heart
The death of a mother and the trauma of a brother
Brought you to your knees asking God, "why?"
Only if you knew that too much space
Breeds insanity.

Only if you knew the love I have for you.

The love I have for you is unimaginable
My king
You are the first man I knew
You are my everything
My flesh and blood
My very own maker

For Us, The Sensitive

My prayer is for you to see life differently again
That love is real
The only thing that helps an aching heart
That you yourself deserve forgiveness
And that you can forgive others
I heard love is not for the weak
But you can start with yourself.

Loving oneself is glorious and
Loving others is easy
When you love yourself.

My Father, My Doctor

Thought vii:

But see, emotions are not
Subject to women.

Men are human, they cry too.

For Us, The Sensitive

To the abuser:

You will suffer pain
That cannot be escaped.

Still, I forgive you, because my Creator did first.

African names are blessings
They are words of wisdom
And hope for the impossible
Names have power
Just like the tongue
They are not just words
They are our guardian angels

Our names tell tales

my name feels real to me
"God comforts me"
i find that in times when it's difficult for me
to understand the world or the things around me,
nothing else comforts me, but God.

your name might mean something
greater than you think.

For Us, The Sensitive

When a woman's husband dies
She should not have to suffer, as she is already in pain
She should be allowed to gain her strength back
She should not be stripped of her wealth
She should be flooded with love and comfort
She should not have to be called a witch
And have to prove she is not the cause of her husband's death
She should be given her husband's wealth
She should not be looked at as a stranger, or a money eater
She should keep her family's riches for herself and her offspring
She should be allowed to mourn peacefully and as she wishes
She brings too much to the table
She brings life to the world
She is life.

This is for Widows in our countries
You are also mothers of all nations
Your strength will never be forgotten.

Thought viii:

Imagine telling someone they hurt you but you are portrayed as a pretender, when you are truly hurting.
This is how the world treats black women when we share our feelings and demand the love we deserve.
Black women deserve love and respect. Give it to them.

If you have privilege, recognize it.

For Us, The Sensitive

I am a woman
Who loves herself enough
To protect her heart
And enough to realize
Life will be lived fully
With or without your love.

Journal entry iv

Hey there,
Remember when you snapped back?
When you healed?
When you were straight?
It was because you did the work.

Now, do the work again.

Sincerely, Tums
Kisses!

For Us, The Sensitive

~~"You have lost/gained weight.~~
~~Are you okay?"~~

I was guilty of
Using such words
Until it was said to me.

My eyes went cloudy
When I heard these words
I saw the destruction
It did to me in seconds.
So, I stopped making comments on people's weight
Because I know the harm it can cause.

Not every word is a compliment
Be careful with your words.

what your mouth cannot say to yourself, don't say to another.

I keep dancing, I never stop
I keep dancing round the circle
Of our endless bittersweet love.

Lovation,
I'm dancing to the beat of your drum
I keep dancing, I never stop.
Is it possible to love a monster?

Some nights, I'm wrapped in your arms
Such a sweet feeling
The arms of a beast
Yet as comfortable as a baby's blanket.

Some nights, I'm weak
Alone and cold
Scared of what might happen again,
Will he hit me...once again?
Then for a second, I think of ending it all
Ending him.

Grab a pillow?
A pot?

For Us, The Sensitive

A knife?
Hit him with a pan?
Stab him?
Poison his food?

What can I do?
Anything to end him.

But then
Does this make me a monster?
Don't we all have some darkness hidden in us?
Hidden in our souls
Waiting to come out and explore evil?

Lovation.

I forgot about love for a second...

Even with this pain,
I think I still love him
Why do I feel this way?
On the floor I lay
Weak from the night before

Bruised and wounded.

I keep loving him,
And I don't know how to stop.

Lovation,
I keep dancing, I never stop
I keep dancing round the circle
Of our endless bitter sweet love
Why can't I just leave?

I was tired
I was weary
A deep realization came to me
Like a sharp ray of light
In the darkness of the night
I felt shame and pain
Empty and guilty
All this while
I thought to myself?
"Why don't you love her?
Tend to her,
Water her garden and see it grow.

For Us, The Sensitive

Serve her and pray for her
Why don't you love yourself?"

I wondered how I could love another
All this while,
Without loving myself first.

As sudden as an April shower
There was a realization of self-love
The evolution of the mind and body
My soul finally breathed.

Lovation,
Developing a deep love for oneself.

I keep dancing, I never intend to stop
I keep dancing round the circle
Of my endless honey sweet love
My ritual became love and personal happiness
I water my garden,
Tend to it
And it grows.

Lovation,
I am dancing to the beat of my drum,
I keep dancing, I won't stop.
At last I love myself
And I won't stop.

Lovation.

For Us, The Sensitive

My country is falling to pieces,

My country is falling to pieces, and we can see it with our eyes.

My country is still falling, can't you see it?

My country is rich, my country is great, but
My country is falling to pieces

Where will I start, and how will I tell you
My country is rich, my country is great, but
My country is falling to pieces and it's an emergency.

As I write this piece
I hear the echoes and woes
Of my exes saying,
"Damn you"
But my pen remains deaf
To the sound of privileged male offspring.
Little do they know
That I have loved harder
Than I ever thought I could
Even while we were in love.

Sorry Not Sorry.

For Us, The Sensitive

With my racing thoughts
And (sometimes) distorted speech
You accept me the way I am.

Thank you for loving me the way I came.

I know this girl named Dami,
She is Yoruba and elegant
Sharp, with a strong voice
A defender of black people
She is a lover and a fighter
Fighting for us glorious black women.

A dancer who is known to be a diva.
Joint rolled up
Hair newly dyed
Shades up
Nails sparkling
Skin glowing
Shoes so fly
Just like herself.

She is conscious,
Aware of herself, her race, her life,
Her struggles and her blessings.
My African Woman,
We see you, keep shining.

The New Nigerian.

For Us, The Sensitive

Look how you forgot
To bring your smile
Your heart
Your courage and your dreams.

Come, let me show you
How the world
Almost broke her bones
And burnt her out
But she has healed herself
At times she thought she could not.

She is a woman,
She brings life
Into the world in every way
Woman,
The most valuable asset on earth.

A Woman

A drop of sun, mixed with honey
A full jar of love, courage and unexplained beauty.
A cup of empathy, sprinkled with tourmalines

Might be threatening to some,
However it's the calmest place to rest your heart.

A Black Woman

For Us, The Sensitive

~ Royal Reminders ~

Things to remember before you forget:

- you're never alone
- cry if you feel
- get some light
- this year is happening once in a your lifetime, don't waste time being unhappy
- overthinking? It never helps
- remove unnecessary emotions that are not yours to feel
- visualize the life you want, then live it
- you're adorbs
- help yourself
- love honestly
- don't substitute your sleep for anything
- you're the wo(man)
- move yourself
- feel
- drink lots of water
- live
- move yourself, again
- no to half love

For Us, The Sensitive

- follow your dreams - they are never too small or big

Have you thought of yourself today?
And the life you bring to the world?
How the sun smiles at you
And the moon sits right at your bedside

Aren't you aware
Of the power of your love
And the beauty of your soul?
Making them wonder
Who you are.

Your Soft-Heartedness Is Striking

For Us, The Sensitive

Journal entry iv:

Overthinking & overanalyzing

*overthinking might lead to losing oneself.
you might wake up one day and don't know who you are
because you have let the opinions of people into your heart.
you then become exactly what they wanted you to be, and
nothing like y***our true self.**

You will find yourself again by **being your own friend** and **communicating with others on how you feel.**

We all need help when we are lost; but **only you can guide yourself all the way back home,** because **only you know who you were,** how you got here, **who you truly want to be,** and **how to find your way back to yourself.**

Sincerely, Tums
Kisses!

Journal entry v:

I don't fancy criticism, but I have learnt to set some boundaries with some words and certain statements so I know when to pay attention to it and when to totally ignore it.
Sometimes criticism can help me correct some mistakes I made and help me grow, but other times it is absolutely useless.
And, it can break you.

Sincerely, Tums

For Us, The Sensitive

When you start learning
You are changing
When you start doing
You are growing

With time, change improves.
It might be what you need
For your life to get better
Not necessarily what you want.

Change will come at each stage
There will be discomfort
However it will get better
It might not be easy to do these things
But love, honesty, patience, healthy boundaries
And understanding is what
All relationships need to survive.

Thought ix:

I have seen that in life
Some friendships do not go
Hand in hand with growth.

Imagine being that friend
Left at the roadside,
Because you are unable to
Grasp the change that
Comes with growing
And the space that
Is needed at times.

My dears,
Take no offence to this
Because there is no love lost.
And do not think you will never
Be that friend to do such.
You might experience certain growth
Which will make you leave
People behind, even family.

For Us, The Sensitive

Still, there is no love lost.

Such is life.

Thought x:

Why do we usually underestimate our value and the gifts Oluwa has blessed us with?
It is silly to think you are not a powerful being, walking on this land of milk and honey.
It is us humans that used our hands to destroy this land
And poisoned our hearts to make us believe that we aren't all powerful.

Who said we can't live as one?
It is us who said we can't live as one
That all fingers are not equal.
But these three together:
Love, Peace and Harmony
Trumps the thirst for power.

With love, I can die for you even
If I don't know your name.

This is what my creator has done for me.

For Us, The Sensitive

Nothing is worse than unconsciously allowing yourself to get hurt because you keep making excuses for the people or things that cause you pain; when you can always make a decision to separate yourself from the situation or the person.

Nothing is worse than knowing you have the power to choose to get hurt (in certain circumstances) but choosing otherwise.
This is what I call a double dose of pain.
It is never a good idea.

So, here's what shame does to you:

it stops you from being who you are
it puts you in a little box
makes you forget who you want to be
it puts you in a hiding place
where you are easily forgotten
shame will steal your dreams
it could steal you away too
don't let it.

no shame in my game

For Us, The Sensitive

Never believe that there is no hope for the love you want. Never believe your standards are too high for the love you deserve.
Never believe the love you deserve does not exist.

Sometimes people tell me it's unrealistic to find yourself.
But when I mean "finding myself", I'm referring to being able to be happy with myself despite out of control situations.

Aren't there some times when one loses themselves?
It is an uncomfortable feeling.
The feeling of not finding joy in your daily routine, making decisions you would typically not make, or letting go of the things you are enthusiastic about.

How do I find myself again?
It is by rediscovering my interests, enjoying my routine, understanding my mistakes, analyzing my choices, forgiving myself, loving my personal time, tracing back my steps and simply starting over, even if I started over last week.

Finding myself is reminding myself of the things that always made me feel at home - the things that kept me sane.

For Us, The Sensitive

It is reminding myself of ME,
and the internal joy I had as a child.

what kind of love makes you forget who you are?
what kind of love makes you have sleepless night?
oh human, what are you doing to yourself?
will you wake up now?

People use Christ as a cover up to judge other humans.

Not knowing anything about your background or experiences, they bring God into it and analyze you, while comparing you to others who are not on your journey.

When God speaks through people, God condemns the sin, not the person.
Don't be deceived by what one man says in the name of Christ.
There are false believers walking around to breed a false version of yourself.

Be your own being in Christ, listen to your creator and search for him in all you do.

Only what the Father thinks of us is what is valid, baby.

You might have missed it somewhere...but now that you know, don't ever let God go.

Journal entry vi

Lonely

Sometimes it gets too lonely for me. I get scared that this will be my life.
But then again, is there anything wrong with that? Maybe it's because I haven't learnt to live by myself and accept the things I run away from.
I haven't learnt to enjoy my company and stay with my own flaws, while loving them too.

It has been hard to accept the things that make me uncomfortable - my thoughts.

I want to be able to enjoy my company, so that when someone walks into my life, they are complementary to the life I already live, rather than having expectations from them.

I don't want a partner to try to fill a void I should be filling.

I want to learn to start loving my 'alone time'. Wear nice lingerie, play some music, read a book, watch a show, dance around my apartment while I cook.

And *on days that are quiet, I hope I have enough joy for myself and those around me.*

Sincerely, Tums
Kisses!

For Us, The Sensitive

Some days are selfcare, but every day is self love.

There are consequences of being an open book.
There are consequences of living your life loud.
There are consequences of sharing your struggles so others can learn and know no pain.

There will always be consequences of being who I am
However, I will walk in who I am because all I've ever wanted was to be free as a bird.

For Us, The Sensitive

I hope we all stop being hypocrites, and start
accepting the people around us for
who they are, while they are here and caring for
their wellness.
Instead of loving them when it's too late.

The feelings you have
have been felt by many.
These emotions that run through you are in the
veins of many.
you are not alone.
Your thoughts, feelings and emotions are valid.

Do you see the constant change in the clouds?
That is the flexibility of your heart,
Also created by God.
It's okay.
Leave your heart as soft as it is.

God's image

The world is NOT better off without you.
perish that thought
now, take a deep breath
and think of the ones that can't live without you
even if they might be the very people that drive you crazy
they are the reason why you know what love is.

now, think of yourself
if you were strong enough to live till this date,
you are powerful enough to live another
and wise enough to understand the problem is not you but our world.
you must dance to your own drum my love, and silence all words of lies
silence the thoughts of deceit and fall in love with your life - no matter the experiences
allow yourself to experience disappointment for a short time, but don't let it take you away.

my love, I don't judge these thoughts because I understand them myself;

For Us, The Sensitive

but your life is too beautiful to be taken to an unknown world, you precious thing.

I love you,
Tums.

Note to self, note to whom it may concern.

Stories to tell:

- first kiss
- first love
- first job
- first drink
- first house
- first words
- first drive
- first big pay
- first award
- first "i love you'
- first child
- heartbreak
- friendship
- spiritual journey
- marriage
- friendship
- a miracle
- embarrassing moment
- a loving bed memory
- lover's trip
- family trip

For Us, The Sensitive

- ❖ a friendship's end
- ❖ self-discovery
- ❖ life discovery
- ❖ adventures
- ❖ wins

__Advice__

my love,
smile - wide
let your joy come from within.

do good things, do enjoyable things and do quality things to stay sane.

give thanks to your creator.

hurt no one.

apologize when wrong.

understand what it means to guard yourself.

enhance your brain and preserve your heart from hate.

being tolerant is powerful,
because it is one of the hardest things to do, so try to be tolerant/patient.

For Us, The Sensitive

love is a gift, and a mixture of every feeling ever felt.

don't punish yourself for things left unsaid, and yesterday's mistakes.

talk to your maker,
tell him your dreams, passions, and feelings.
be kind to everyone, even if you deem them undeserving.
have faith, and trust yourself

learn from your mistakes

love your heart as it is.

love yourself
and love all.

Words I'd love to tell my children to live by...

Affirmations/Aide mémoire

These affirmations are first-person and third-person statements that serve as a memory aid. They encourage self confidence and a positive mindset, which creates space for manifestation and peace of mind.
I hope these statements inspire you.

i.
I have forgiven myself because I love myself.
I have forgiven myself because I am creating a space for blessings.
Despite my past, I can be a better version of myself.

ii.
I deserve to spend time on the things I enjoy. I deserve time to myself and time to recharge.

iii.
I shall let go of any thoughts of comparison and trust my journey on earth to serve my soul and to serve God.

iv.
God has blessed me with gifts, and I will use them to flourish in this land of the living.

v.
No matter what I experience, I will be compassionate to those around me and to myself.

vi.
I have control over negative words, thoughts and feelings. I have power over anger and sadness.

vii.
I love the human I have grown to be. I am growing into my own being.
I am beautifully carved in every area of my life.

viii.

I am healthy in my body and I am healthy in my soul. I am healthy in my mind and I am whole.

xi.

I have the courage to walk away from things that don't serve my heart. I love my peace and I love my life.

x.

I am more than what society labels me. I am a graceful individual and an extraordinary human.

END NOTE:

I wrote this book with a significant amount of joy in my heart, wanting you to know that you are special.

You can be as soft as a feather or hard as rock and still be lovable.

You can conquer all things, even the voice of your personal saboteur.
You are powerful and I wish you joyful days ahead.

Love, Tumi.

Special Thanks

To my editor Temi Boyede, thank you for coming on this journey with me.
Lots of love.

www.ingramcontent.com/pod-product-compliance
Lightning Source LLC
Chambersburg PA
CBHW030307100526
44590CB00012B/552